Prayers
for
Parents

Renee Bartkowski

Liguori
ONE LIGUORI DRIVE
LIGUORI MO 63057-9999

Imprimi Potest:
Richard Thibodeau, C.Ss.R.
Provincial, Denver Province
The Redemptorists

ISBN 0-7648-0687-4
Library of Congress Catalog Card Number: 00-104094

To order, call 1-800-325-9521
www.liguori.org
www.catholicbooksonline.com

Cover design by Wendy Barnes

CONTENTS

4. Teaching My Children

5. Encouraging My Own Growth

6. Relating to My Children

7. Daily Life

8. Family Life

9. Facing Adolescence

10. Preparing for Life

11. Dealing with Other People

12. Special Situations

Introduction

One of the most difficult—and most important—jobs on this earth is that of bringing up a child. And yet, it is a job for which many of us are not well trained.

Most of us usually step into parenthood relying on our own intuition—and perhaps on what our parents have taught us. However, our intuition is sometimes flawed and our emotions often interfere with our good judgment. As a result, we often end up making mistakes.

This prayer book can serve as a mini-course in parenting by bringing to mind concepts that we should all be teaching our children. The prayers, which may be used by either single or married parents, present suggestions not only on how to handle specific situations that we encounter as parents but also on how to build strong, trusting, and amiable relationships with our children.

These prayers can also help us to connect with the wisest parent of all—our Father in heaven—who is always ready and willing to give us the strength, the patience, and the wisdom we need to be able to mold our children into good, responsible, and loving adults.

ONE

BEING A PARENT

Appreciating My Most Important Job

Lord, I spend my days rushing busily from my job
    to chores at home
        to obligations in my community—
            always anxiously struggling to do all the things
                I feel I ought to be doing.
    And when it's time to be with my children
        I'm often totally drained
            and exhausted.

Sometimes I feel as if I'm giving them
        only leftover pieces of my time and energy.

Don't let me ever forget, Lord,
        that out of all the jobs I have to do,
            right now—at this time in my life—
                parenting is the most important.

Being a success at work or in my community
    will mean little if I'm not a success as a parent.

Remind me, Lord,
    to refocus my attention and conserve my energy
        for this most important job of mine.

Let me be constantly aware
        of how great a privilege it is
            to be entrusted with bringing up these children.

How blessed I am to have you think
        that I am worthy of this responsibility.

Don't let me make a mess of it, Lord.
    Help me to do a good job with these fragile souls
        whom you have entrusted to my care.

Being a Pal

There are times when—
  in my desire to be liked by my children—
    I act like a pal instead of a parent.

Remind me, Lord, that my children need a parent—
    not just another pal.

They need a parent
  who will take the lead and guide them—
  who will never hesitate to say "no" to them
      when the need arises—
  who will make rules and set boundaries
      to keep them from doing wrong.

I want my children to feel the security of knowing
  that someone who is deeply concerned about them
      is always in charge.

I want to provide them with a stable and safe harbor
  from which they can venture out and deal with
      the stresses and challenges of life.

Remind me, Lord, that—
  although I can and should listen
      to their views and opinions—
    it is I who must ultimately guide their actions
        and keep them on course—
      even when they rebel against me,
      even when they get upset with me
          and say they don't like me.

Being a Vigilant Parent

Lord, help me to be a parent
          who is always vigilant and aware.

There's so much in this world
          that can harm my children.

There's so much for me to keep up with—
     the programs they're watching on television,
     the books they're reading,
     the music they're listening to,
     the friends they're associating with.
          It's so hard to monitor everything.

Sometimes it just seems easier
     to let them do what they want
          as long as they stay busy and contented
               and out of my hair.

Oh, Lord, don't let me ever be tempted to develop
     such a hands-off, don't-care attitude.

Let me remember that my children are not
     mature enough yet to decide for themselves
          just what's good and what's bad.

Help me to be constantly aware of their interests.
     Alert me when they become involved
          in things that are wrong for them.

Keep me on my toes, Lord, and make me
          a good, responsible, and vigilant parent.

Dealing with My Mistakes

Lord, give me the wisdom,
    the confidence, and the strength I need
        to bring my children up well.

There are times when I actually lose faith
        in my ability to be a good parent.

Looking back, I can see
    that I have made a lot of mistakes.
        I have so many regrets.

At times I even wonder if my mistakes
    will—in some way—
        make life harder for my children.

Help me, Lord, not to get discouraged
    with my occasional errors in judgment.

Let me realize that no parent is perfect.
    Being human, we all make mistakes.

Keep reminding me, Lord,
    that you never asked us to be perfect.
        You simply asked us to be loving.

So increase my capacity to love, Lord,
    and let my love—and your love—
        make up for the mistakes
            I sometimes make.

Indulging My Need for Patience

There are times, Lord,
  when I need a whopping dose of patience.

Give me the patience I need
  to listen to my children's whining—
    and not give in to it.

Give me the patience
  to discipline them
    when they make it difficult for me to do so.

Give me the patience I need
  to witness their squabbles and disagreements
    and always deal with them fairly.

Give me the patience I need
  to repeatedly forgive them
    when they upset me or hurt me.

Give me the patience
  to take the time to listen to their problems
    when I'm overwhelmed with problems of my own.

Give me the patience
  to spend time with them
    when I have a hundred other things to do.

Give me the patience
  to comfort and console them
    when I feel tired and distraught
      and in need of comfort myself.

Oh, Lord, give me the patience I need
  to love them
    when their actions are totally unlovable.

Parenting Is Difficult

Oh, Lord, you know that I feel
    both blessed and thankful
        for the privilege of being a parent,
    but there are times
        when I can't help but wonder
            why you made this job of parenting
            so hard.

I sometimes feel like just sitting down
        and giving in to total discouragement.

At times all I want is peace at any price—
    even at the price of letting down
      on the discipline
        my children so desperately need.

Each year—each month—I keep thinking
    that, as they get older,
        my job will get easier—
    but, as time goes on, all we seem to do
      is to trade one set of difficulties
        for another.

Don't let me get discouraged with it all, Lord.

Give me the strength, the determination,
    and the positive attitude I need
      to do this job really well.
Dear Lord, I'm depending on your help.

TWO

Developing Spirituality

Instilling Spirituality

Help me, Lord, to instill a deep sense of spirituality
        into the lives of my children.

Lately our life together seems to have become
                so compartmentalized.

We tend to completely separate
    the spiritual part of it
        from all the other events that occur each day.

Give me the wisdom and faith I need
    to help my children develop a spirituality
        that permeates every part of their daily lives.

Let me be able to help them understand
    that their chores, their studies, their problems,
        their kindness to others, even their playtime
            are all things that can be done for you,
                shared with you,
                    and offered to you.

Let me be able to show them
    that you are a presence in their lives—
        always there, ready and willing
            to strengthen and comfort them—
    that you are a constant companion
        who can be called upon at any hour of the day
            for support and guidance and help.

I ask you to draw them close to you, Lord,
    so they may never feel alone
        or frightened
        or powerless.

Being a Child of God

I often feel sorry for myself
  when my children misbehave
          and disappoint me.

Remind me, Lord, that you, too,
  have to deal with us—
      your children—
  who often fail to do right
    and end up disappointing you.

Help me, Lord,
  to get through each day
      without disappointing you.

Teaching Them to Pray

Lord, help me to teach my children how to pray—
    to teach them that a prayer
        is not just something that is said before meals—
            or before climbing into bed in the evening—
                but at any time of the day or night.

Let me be able to show them how to make their prayers
    into intimate conversations in which they can share
        every part of their daily lives with you.

Let me be able to inspire them
    to speak to you often throughout the day—
    to whisper a short prayer of gratitude
        when they happen to witness a beautiful sunset—
        or when something nice occurs in their lives.

Or to occasionally just stop and say,
    "I'm having a good time, Lord. Share it with me."

Let me be able to teach them
    that they can ask for your help when they're troubled—
        for your guidance when they're confused—
        and for your comfort when they're frightened.

Let me always remind them to say, "I'm sorry, Lord,"
    when they happen to do something wrong.

Help me to also teach them the value of praying
    for others—
    for their family, their friends,
        for those who are less fortunate than they are.

Dear Lord, give me the ability to show them
    how to make prayer into a daily day-long habit.

Relying on God As My Partner

My battery really needs recharging, Lord.

There are days when I get so tired and exhausted
    that I feel as if I just won't have enough strength
        to go on facing the many demands of parenthood.

If only I could take a day off
    to just sit quietly at your feet
        and have you energize me.

Lord, I shall stop for a moment—right now—
    to ask you to let me feel your presence.

Help me to feel secure in the knowledge
    that you are always available with your help.

I want you to know that I desperately need
    your guidance.

I pray that you will fill me with your peace,
        your strength, and your wisdom.

When the going gets rough, remind me, Lord,
    that you are always at my side ready to help me.

Remind me that—with you as my partner—
    I can be a really good and successful parent.

THREE

Facing Life

Balancing Space and Support

There are times, Lord,
>   when I want not merely to guide my children.
>>   Instead, I get overwhelmed with this driving desire
>>   to completely direct their lives.

I often find myself actually hovering over them—
>   ready to jump in with my advice
>>   on when, where, and how they ought to do things.
>   And when something goes wrong,
>>   I'm usually ready to rush to their rescue
>>   and fix things up for them.

How can they possibly become
>   mature, responsible, and independent individuals,
>>   if I'm always there to direct
>>>   every little part of their lives?

Keep reminding me, Lord, that my children
>   need a little healthy space in which to grow.

Let me be wise enough to know
>   when it's time to give advice and support—
>   and when it's time to just back off
>>   and let them try to do things on their own.

Help me, Lord, to always strike a good balance
>   between space and support.

Fostering Satisfaction

Remind me, Lord, that one of the greatest gifts
    I can pass on to my children
        is a sense of satisfaction with their lives.

I know that I will never be able to accomplish this
    if I fall into the habit of openly expressing
        dissatisfaction with my own life.

Remind me, Lord, to always go out of my way
    to show my children that,
        even though there are occasional problems,
            I can accept life as it is.

Let me be able to show them that I have the ability
        to always focus on the good instead of the bad.

Help me to develop the habit of making my children
    deeply aware of all the good things in their lives.

Remind me to take every opportunity
    to be outspokenly grateful
        for all the small blessings we enjoy each day—
            for our home, our family, our friends.

Don't let me ever say or do anything
    that might encourage them
        to be jealous of what others have—
            or to long for things that we don't or can't have.

Lord, give me the ability to teach my children
    to fully recognize, appreciate, and be thankful
        for their talents, their relationships,
and all the privileges and opportunities that are theirs.

Let me always seek ways to show them
    how really blessed and fortunate we are.

Responsibility for Our Actions

Remind me, Lord, to always teach my children
   that they are fully responsible for their actions.

Let me be able to make them understand
   that we are each totally accountable
      for all the things we do and say—
      and that we cannot excuse ourselves
         by blaming others for our actions,
      ` for no one can make us do wrong
         unless we choose to allow them to.

Dear Lord, let me also be able to show them
   that all of their actions have consequences
      that they will have to face and endure.

Don't let me ever be tempted to excuse them
   when I see them doing wrong—
      or when I'm told by others
         that they've done something wrong.

Make me realize that there may be times
   when I must simply stand by and
      let them suffer the consequences of their actions,
         no matter how much it hurts them—or me.

Remind me, Lord,
   that they will grow up to be better individuals
      if they learn that they must always
         answer for their own actions.

Building Self-confidence

Give me the wisdom I need, Lord,
    to help each of my children develop
        a strong feeling of self-confidence.

Let me be able to inspire them
    to have faith in themselves—
    to fully appreciate their assets and talents
        and not be discouraged by their limitations.

Let me be able to encourage them
        to work with whatever abilities they have—
    and never fall into the habit
        of comparing themselves with others
        or of being jealous of the talents
                that others possess.

Help them to understand, Lord,
            that you—and I—
                love them just as they are.

Let them realize that you want each of them
    to appreciate their own uniqueness and specialness
        and merely do the best they can
            with whatever they have.

Developing the Right Attitudes

Lord, help me impress my children with the fact
   that not only are they each totally in charge
      of choosing their own attitudes toward life—
   but also that choosing the right attitudes
      can make their lives easier
         and much more pleasant.

Let them be able to see that, when things go wrong,
   they can choose to react positively
            with acceptance and adjustability—
      or negatively
            with resentment and self-pity.

When someone hurts or angers them,
   they can choose to be forgiving and understanding—
   or they can be vengeful and unpardoning.

When they don't get their own way,
   they can choose to whine and be crabby—
      or to put on a smile and make the best of things.

Lord, give me the ability to show them
   that only they can decide whether they want
      to be unhappy, negative, complaining people,
         whom others would rather avoid—
      or to be happy, positive, forward-looking people,
         with whom others would like to associate.

Dear Lord, help them to make the right choices.

FOUR

Teaching My Children

Handling Problems

Give me the wisdom I need, Lord,
  to be able to teach my children
    how to handle problems.

Let me be able to help them understand
  that problems are merely a normal part
    of everyday life
    that must be met and faced by everyone—
  and that most problems can eventually be resolved
    without giving in to worry and despair.

Help me to show them
    that problems don't usually have to be faced alone,
  if only they remain willing to ask
      for the advice and support of others.

Lord, let me also be able
  to help my children understand that,
    although not all problems have solutions,
      it is possible to live through difficult—
        and even tragic—situations
          with courage and faith.

I want to be able to teach them, Lord,
  that you are constantly at their sides,
      always ready to guide and strengthen them
    if only they ask for and have faith
        in your presence and in your help.

Lord, give me the wisdom I need
        to be able to teach my children
  that problems are best handled
      when they are handled in partnership with you.

Handling Failures

Help me, Lord, to teach my children
    how to accept and deal with their failures.

Don't let their occasional failures
    discourage them or depress them.

Let me be able to show them
    that it's not necessarily bad to fail—
        as long as they've tried to do their best
        and are willing to try again.

Help me to teach them to regard a failed project
    as an opportunity for learning and growing—
    to view it not as an obstacle
        but as a steppingstone to success.

Dear Lord, let my children grow up
    to be strong and resilient
        in the face of difficulties and defeats.

Give them the confidence
    and determination they'll need
        to always pick themselves up and try again.

And let me always remember, Lord,
    to praise them not as much for their successes
        as for their effort and willingness
            to at least try to accomplish things.

Teaching Forgiveness

Lord, give me the ability
　　to teach my children to be forgiving.

There are times when someone has wronged them
　　that I am tempted to openly show
　　　　the anger and resentment that I feel
　　　　　　toward those who have hurt them.

Remind me, Lord,
　　that I can do more harm than good
　　　　by displaying such negative reactions.

Don't let me ever be guilty
　　of saying or doing anything
　　　　that would encourage them to hang on
　　　　　　to resentments—
　　　　　　　　or to be vengeful and vindictive.

Let me be able to teach them how to overlook
　　　　the occasional thoughtlessness of others—
　　and to be big enough and kind enough
　　　　to respond with understanding and forgiveness.

Let me also be able to teach them
　　to apologize when they are guilty of hurting others—
　　　　to apologize quickly and sincerely.

Help me to make them understand
　　that two of the nicest, kindest,
　　　　most soothing phrases they can say to others are
　　　　　　"I'm sorry"
　　　　　　　　and "I forgive you."

Imparting the Value of Work

Lord, give me the ability to teach my children
 the value of being diligent and hard working.

Let me be able to impress them with the knowledge
  that life in this world is not always easy—
and that if they want their dreams to come true
  they must be willing to work hard for them.

Help me to make them understand that it takes
  a lot of studying,
   a lot of determination,
    and a lot of practice
 to be able to do things well enough
   to become successful at them.

Let me also be able to impress them with the fact
  that life doesn't owe them anything—
and that what they get out of life
 will be in proportion only
  to what they are willing to put into it.

Dear Lord, give me the wisdom I need
 to be able to make my children understand
  that life does not hand out trophies
   to those who are not willing
    to work for them.

Avoiding Self-pity

When things go wrong for me, Lord,
    I often end up feeling totally sorry for myself.

At times I'm even tempted
    to give in to discouragement
        and actually wallow for a while
            in a pool of self-pity.

What a terrible example to set for my children!

Lord, let me be wise enough and strong enough
    to be able to show my children
        that, although daily life has its ups and downs,
    it's always possible to get through the downs of life
        without succumbing to discouragement
            and self-pity.

Let me be able to teach them
    how to work their way through the bad times
        by focusing more willingly and positively
            on the many good things in their lives.

Dear Lord, grant my children
    the strength and wisdom they'll need
        to be able to get through the difficult
            and discouraging events in their lives
                without feeling sorry for themselves.

Avoiding Greed

I have often watched my children
   speedily tear open Christmas and birthday gifts
      and before they even show their appreciation
         their covetous little eyes
            immediately turn away and look around
            for more.

Show me, Lord, how to teach them
            to be less greedy and more grateful.

It's really hard to accomplish this
   with all the TV commercials
   constantly enticing them—
   and with their friends showing off
      their new possessions to them.

Help me, Lord, to be able to keep them
            from developing a gimme attitude.

Let me realize that at times
   it's good to say "no" to the desires of our children.

We don't do them a favor by constantly trying
            to fulfill their every little wish.

Remind me, Lord, to teach them
   that unfulfilled desires
      are often a normal part of everyone's life.

Dear Lord, let me be able to instill in my children
   not only a deep sense of gratitude
            for anything they receive,
   but also a strong desire to make others happy
            through their own giving.

Teaching Sportsmanship

Lord, I want to be able to develop
 a sense of fairness and good sportsmanship
  in my children,
  but in today's world
   the emphasis seems to be on winning.

Don't let my children be dazzled solely by victories.
 And don't let me ever be guilty, Lord,
  of nurturing superstar egos in them.

Let me be able to show them
 how to keep a proper and healthy perspective
  in regard to their competitive activities.

Let me always do everything I can
 to help them develop
  a good team spirit
   and a sense of joy in participating.

And let me always make sure that I sincerely praise
  the effort and good will they show,
 instead of allowing myself
  to get overly excited about their victories.

Help me, Lord, to be able to instill in them
 a sense of fair play and good sportsmanship
  that will carry over into all aspects
   of their future lives.

FIVE

Encouraging
My Own Growth

Opening My Heart to My Children

There are times, Lord, when my children's behavior
    makes me feel totally frustrated and annoyed.

It's hard not to behave irritably
    and impatiently with them
        when they misbehave and whine and pout.
        At times it's even hard to like them.

Whenever I'm overcome
    with such negative feelings toward them,
    remind me, Lord, of all the precious moments of joy
        they have given me in the past.

Remind me of the warm feeling I've had
    when I've tucked them into bed for the night—
    when I've held them on my lap and read to them—
    when we've gone out to gaze at the stars together.

Remind me of the love I've been privileged to experience
    when they've offered me a radiant smile—
    or presented me with a wilted wildflower—
    or planted an unexpected wet kiss on my cheek.

Oh, Lord, how thankful I am
    that I have these frequently misbehaving,
            naughty,
                exasperating,
                interesting,
                    huggable,
                        lovable
    little people in my life.

Giving Them Roots and Wings

Lord, there are times when—
   in my desire to keep my children
      from hurting themselves—
        I tend to become much too protective.

I know that I must use discretion
      and protect them from dangerous situations,
but remind me, Lord,
   that, in my earnest desire for safety and caution,
      I may run the risk
        of making them afraid of things.

Don't let me be so overprotective
   that I make them afraid to eagerly and willingly
      meet new challenges and experiences.

Don't let me ever say anything to make them too timid
      to accept and face life's many risks.

Let me be able to teach them
   to always look forward to life's adventures
      with wings of eagerness and determination
      and with roots of confidence.

Learning to Trust

There are times when I tend to be quite a worrier, Lord.
  I often fuss and fret not only about serious things,
    but also about small problems.

Remind me, Lord, that it's very easy
      to pass this bad habit on to my children.

I often go out of my way to advise them
    to take their problems to you, Lord,
        and to trust that you will help them.
  Help me to take my own advice.

Dear Lord, don't let me teach my children
        to become worrywarts.

Let me be able to help them develop
    a more positive and confident manner
      of facing life.

Let me be able to show them
    how to turn to you for aid
      and to trust that you will eventually
        guide and help them with their problems.

Lord, give me the temperament I need
    to help them develop
      not only a strong and trusting faith
    in their own ability to face the challenges of life,
      but also a strong and trusting faith in you.

Empowering Them

Lord, I find myself constantly wanting
    to protect my children from making mistakes.
        As a result, I often end up
            making too many decisions for them.

How can I expect them to learn
    how to make decisions throughout their lives,
        if they don't get some practice now?

I know that I must guide them
        and try to keep them from doing wrong—
    but remind me that I cannot and should not
    take it upon myself
        to completely solve all their dilemmas.

Let me learn how to give helpful advice
    and then to be quiet and patient
        and give them the time they need
            to make their own decisions.

When you entrusted us with a free will, Lord,
    you knew that we'd make mistakes,
        but you also knew
            that we'd often learn from our mistakes.

Let me be able to give my children
    some of the same freedom that you have given us.

Help me, Lord, to nurture their independence
    by allowing them to make their own decisions—
        and even their own mistakes.

Fostering Gratitude

Lord, it's so easy for children to learn
    to become whiners and complainers,
        especially if they have a parent
            who frequently complains about things.

Help me, Lord, to always be fully aware
    of any negative views and attitudes I may have—
        and grant me the ability
            to control my expression of them.

I so often catch myself complaining
        in the presence of my children.

I complain about the chores I have to do—
    about things that don't work out as I want them to.

I complain about other people,
    about the weather, about my job,
        about my inability to afford things that I want.

I often don't realize just how much
        complaining I do in front of them.

Lord, I don't want my children to grow up
        with a negative, dissatisfied view of life.

Teach me, Lord, to shift my focus
    away from my discontent
    and to be more openly grateful for all my blessings.

Help me to foster a more positive and contented
        attitude in my children.

Setting Healthy Boundaries for Anger

It's so easy to get angry—even furious—
    with my children, Lord—
especially when I feel tired and overworked.

There are times when they're so exasperating
    that they're able to send my emotions
        into a tailspin.

At times I just let my anger
        get totally out of control,
and I end up shouting and yelling
    and saying things that
        I know I shouldn't say.

I realize that anger is sometimes justified
    and that it's all right for my children
        to observe my anger
        when they do something wrong,
but I don't like myself
        when I let it get out of control.

I certainly don't want to teach them
    that shouting and yelling at one another
        is a good way to handle anger and frustrations.

Give me the strength and patience I need, Lord,
    to be able to handle my anger
        in a much calmer, more mature manner
        so I can set a better example
            for my children to follow.

SIX

Relating to
My Children

Dealing with Perfection

Lord, we often have an image
of just how our children should be—
and when they don't live up to that image
we're tempted to be disappointed with them.

Don't let me ever say or do anything
that would make any of my children feel
that I'm disappointed
with who or what they are.

I know that, as a parent,
I must try to correct their faults
and encourage them to improve themselves—
but in doing so,
don't let me ever give them the impression
that I love them any less
because of their faults and failures.

I don't ever want them to think
that they have to be perfect to be loved.

Teaching by Example

It's so easy to be swayed by permissive philosophies
    and to rationalize some of our
        not-so-nice, not-so-right actions.

Give me the wisdom and strength I need, Lord,
    not only to live according to your teachings
        with a true and unyielding
            sense of right and wrong—
    but to also be able to pass
        the right values and principles on to my children.

Remind me, Lord,
        that I must always practice what I preach,
    for my children are very observant and can be easily
            influenced by the things they see me do—
        such as telling a small lie to a friend—
        or not being completely honest at the
            supermarket—
        or taking part in a bit of unkind gossip
            about a neighbor.

Whenever I'm tempted to act contrary
        to what I truly believe and teach,
    remind me, Lord,
        that my children are in greater need of a model
            than of a preacher.

Dealing with Different Personalities

How in the world did I ever manage to raise
        such totally different children?
I've always tried to treat them the same,
    but each one reacts so differently
        to my discipline and criticism and praise.

Lord, give me the wisdom I need
    to understand their differences
        and to know how to deal with each of them.

I must admit that there are times
    when I wish that one were more like another.

There are even times when it's much easier
    to love one more than another.

Oh, Lord, don't let me ever be guilty
    of favoring one over another—
        or of comparing them with each other.

Help me to avoid saying or doing anything
    that would make them think they have to compete
        with each other for my love and approval.

Let me always be able to see and appreciate
    the uniqueness and specialness of each child—
    and to love each one as fully and completely
        as each needs to be loved.

Keep reminding me, Lord, that it is often the most
    disobedient, rebellious, hard-to-love child
        who needs the most love and acceptance.

Oh, Lord, help me to be able
    to make each of my children feel special—
        and totally and completely loved.

Communicating Wisely

Lord, give me the wisdom
   and understanding I need
      to know how to communicate with my children.

I must admit that there are times
   when I tend to be too preachy and overbearing—
      or too quick to criticize and correct.

Sometimes I even forget that good communication
   consists of both speaking and listening.

And I often fail to take the time to really listen—
   to try to discover and understand
      what my children are thinking and feeling.

Lord, give me the ability to always listen to them
      with an open mind and heart.

Remind me of how easy it is to turn them completely off
   by being overly critical and disapproving
      of their views and their choices.

Let me be able to foster a relationship between us
   that will make them want
      to share their experiences with me—
         and to listen to and trust my advice.

And don't let me ever forget, Lord,
   that communication with children
      does not usually wait for a convenient time—
   for a time when I happen to be in the mood
      or not too busy or distracted by other things.

Let me learn to be available to them
      when they feel the need to talk.

Loving Them

It's so easy to love my children
        when they're obedient
                and sweet and loving.

Help me to love them, Lord,
        when they're whining
                and pouting and misbehaving.

Teach me, Lord, how to love them
        when they're difficult to love.

Remind me that at times
        we are all difficult to love.

Praising Wisely

Lord, in my effort to develop
     a good sense of self-esteem in my children,
       I sometimes find myself
         going overboard with my praise.

I know that they really need
    my praise and encouragement,
      but let me be careful not to overdo it.

Let me be able to teach them
    that praise must be earned.

Remind me, Lord, that there is nothing wrong
    in letting them know that I won't be satisfied
      with a chore that's sloppily done—
       or with school work that does not reflect
        an earnest attempt to do the best they can.

Let me realize that I won't be doing them a favor
    by accepting work that's done
      with an uncaring attitude
       or a minimum of effort.

Let me remember
    that they must begin learning now
      that success in this world is achieved
        only through hard work and diligent effort.

They must learn that when they go out in the world
    praise will not usually be profusely showered
      upon them for each little job they do.

Teach me, Lord, how to always keep a good balance
    between criticism and praise.

Dealing with the Stages of Growth

From the terrible twos to the rebellious teens—
    it's often such a struggle to get through
        each of the many difficult stages of growth!

I sometimes find myself not only getting frustrated
    and discouraged with the negative side of each stage,
        but also actually dreading each future phase.

Lord, let me learn to lighten up a bit and realize
    that, in growing up, it is necessary for my children
        to work their way through the difficulties
          and challenges of each stage of life.

Sometimes they do well—
    and sometimes they don't—
        and I find myself wondering just how
          we'll survive it all.

Lord, help me to face all these growing pains
        with a more positive attitude.

Let me realize that it is through these struggles
    that our children learn to eventually
        stand on their own two feet.

Give me the ability, Lord, to enjoy my children
    in each of these periods of growth and adjustment.

Let me learn how to actually savor and take pleasure
    in the many challenges of each phase.

Our children grow up too soon, don't they, Lord?

Too soon we'll look back and miss all these struggles!

SEVEN

Daily Life

Establishing Priorities

Like most parents, I often try to inspire my children
   to strive for a successful and secure life.

In doing so, however,
   I sometimes find myself inadvertently
      putting too much emphasis
         on the material things of life.

Nowadays it's so easy
   to end up giving them the impression
      that success is equated
         with money and possessions.

Lord, let me be more careful
   of what I really teach them.

Give me the wisdom I need
      to help them keep their priorities straight.

Let me be able to foster in them
   a sense of what is really important
         for a successful and happy life—
      their faith in you—
      their relationships with family and friends—
      their sense of achievement and service—
      and the security of knowing that they themselves
         are good, kind, nice people
            who both love and are loved.

Disciplining Effectively

Lord, give me the wisdom I need
        to be a good and fair disciplinarian.

Let me always be able to strike a good balance
        between being too rigid and too lenient.

At times it's really hard to tell
    just how tough I should be.

Grant me the ability to know
    when it's important and necessary
        to put my foot down and be firm—
and when it's better
        to refrain from coming down too hard on them.

Lord, teach me how to discipline with an easiness
        that shows my love and understanding—
and yet with a toughness
        that will bring out the best in my children.

And keep reminding me, Lord, of how important
        and necessary it is to be consistent.

Give me the perseverance I need
    to always follow through
        when trying to teach my children to behave.

Dear Lord, let me be able to make them understand
    that the limits I set on their behavior
        are set not because I wish
            to make their lives more difficult,
but only because I love them
    and care about them
        and want to make their lives safer and better.

Taming Our Busy Schedules

Lord, there are times when I just can't believe
      how overscheduled our lives have become.

We rush zealously from soccer to swimming
      to baseball to dancing.
   We coach and watch and cheer and applaud.

We often push and prod our children
   into participating in a frantic whirl of activity.
     And then we end up wondering if perhaps
      there's too much regimentation
      and competition in their lives.

I know that it's good for children to learn
      to develop their physical skills
 and to have the experience
   of playing and working together as a team,
 but let me remember
   that they also need time to just be kids—
   to relax and enjoy the pleasures of childhood.

They need time to be in charge
   of planning and running their own activities—
   to have their own kind of fun with their friends—
   and even to occasionally just be alone and daydream.

They need time to think things out for themselves
   and to develop their own resources and imaginations.

Lord, let me always remember to be careful
      not to push them too hard.

Criticizing Wisely

There are so many times, Lord,
    when it's necessary to reprimand my children
        for doing something wrong.

When I must scold them,
    let me always remember to criticize the act—
        not the child.

Don't let me ever be guilty
    of giving them the impression
        that they are bad or ignorant or unlovable.

Let me be able to show them
    that it is not they themselves
        but their behavior
            that is wrong and unacceptable.

I ask you, Lord, to give me the wisdom I need
    to know how to keep my criticism
        from being degrading or demeaning.

Don't let anything I say ever damage
    my children's sense of worth and self-esteem.

Let me have the ability to know how to criticize
    constructively rather than destructively.

And whenever I must criticize them,
    remind me, Lord, to always take time afterward
        to reassert my unconditional love for them.

Monitoring Television Time

Lord, it's so tempting to use the television set
    as a baby-sitter.

It makes life so much easier if I can simply allow
    my children to just sit back and be entertained
        while I go about my chores
            in relative peace and quiet.

Don't let me be tempted, Lord, to encourage
    my kids to become television addicts.

Help me to use good judgment in limiting the time
    I allow them to spend in front of the set.

And give me the wisdom I need, Lord,
    to be able to choose programs for them
        that are inspiring and wholesomely entertaining.

Let me be alert enough
    to keep them from being exposed
        to some of the mind-numbing, mind-corrupting junk
        that is often aired on television.

I know that it takes a bit of time and effort
    to screen their programs
        and set boundaries for them to follow.

Let me be willing, Lord,
    to take the time not only to do this important job
    but also to discuss with them
        any of the harmful and improper things
        they may happen to see or wish to see.

Lord, give me the determination I need
    to always stand firm in my restrictions—
        despite any objections that may follow.

Making Life Easy

I often catch myself wanting to make things
        easy and pleasant for my children.

How will they ever learn what real life is like
    if I don't ever allow them to struggle and stumble—
        and even fall at times?

Remind me, Lord, that there are times
    when I should step back
        and just let them take their knocks in life.

I should allow them to skin their knees and stub their toes
    and feel all the lumps and bumps of everyday living.

For their own good,
        they must learn that life is not easy—
           nor is it always fair—
           nor does it always turn out the way we want it to.

Let me be careful, Lord,
        to avoid constantly running interference for them—
    to refrain from rushing to help them
        when they're habitually running late—
    to avoid making excuses for them
        when they do something wrong—
    to keep from finishing a project for them
        when they run out of time
        or simply fail to put their best into it.

Let me be tough enough, Lord,
        to allow them to struggle and strain
           and experience occasional failures.

And I pray, Lord, that you'll watch over them
    and help them to learn from all their struggles.

EIGHT

Family Life

Developing Family Spirit

Help me, Lord, to be able to instill in my children
>> a sense of love and loyalty for our family.

Let me be able to make them understand
>> that a family is a team,
>>> and we are all team players.

As such, we are each equally important contributors
> to the success and well-being of our life as a family.

Give me the wisdom I need, Lord,
>> to be able to teach them the value
>>> of cooperation, compromise, and sharing.

Let me be able to inspire them
>> to be supportive rather than competitive—
>> to be forgiving rather than vengeful—
>> to be understanding rather than argumentative—
>> and to be concerned for others
>>> rather than self-centered.

Help them to understand
>> that each of us is responsible
>>> for the peace and happiness in our home.

Dear Lord, let them realize how fortunate we all are
>> to be part of a loving and caring family.

Dealing with Sibling Rivalry

Why—oh, why, Lord, do siblings fight so much?

I often watch my children arguing and teasing
   and taking their frustrations out on each other.

I hear them saying hurtful things to one another—
   and it just breaks my heart!

Dear Lord, whenever it becomes necessary for me
   to step in and referee their arguments,
      please help me to handle it correctly.

I often feel that I need the wisdom of Solomon
   to be truly fair and impartial.

Help me, Lord, to avoid falling into the trap
   of judging one child more harshly than another—
   or of interfering too quickly in their skirmishes.

Give me the knowledge and the patience I need
   to be able to show them
      how to settle their own arguments
         with cooperation and compromise,
      how to overcome
         their jealousies and their competitiveness.

And help them to understand
   how much they hurt each other
      with their bickering and their attitudes of revenge.

Dear Lord, give me the ability to inspire my children
   to see the importance and the preciousness
      of building relationships for the future
         that are free of envy and anger.

Let me be able to teach them how to truly love
   one another.

Establishing Family Chores

Sometimes it's easier to just do a job myself
    than to argue with my children
        about getting their daily chores done.

Remind me, Lord, that I can't possibly instill
    good work habits in them by taking over and
        allowing them to shirk their responsibilities.

Help me to make them understand
    that each person in a family is responsible
        for contributing to the smooth running
           of a household—
    that it is necessary for each of us
        to do our fair share of chores—
           even those that are the most tedious
           and least liked.

Help me to make them understand
    that we cannot always do
        only the things we like to do.

Give me the wisdom and patience, Lord,
    to instill in my children
        not only a sense of duty to family life,
        but also a respect for good, honest work.

Treasuring Magic Moments

Lord, don't let me ever miss an opportunity
    to bond with my children in one of those
        magic moments of parenting.

In my rush to get things done,
    I sometimes come close to missing out
        on special moments with my children—
    those precious moments that are worth capturing
      and treasuring in the corners of our hearts.

Remind me to always take the time
      to share such intimate moments with them—
    to lie in the grass and watch the clouds drift by—
    to go out at night and gaze at the stars—
    to build a snowman together—
    to go dancing in the rain.

Let me go out of my way to make the time
      to plan and do simple special things with them—
    to have a picnic on a blanket in the living room
        on a cold winter's evening—
    to lie down in bed with them
        and make up silly songs together.

Let me be able to give them
    secure and intimate memories
      that they can cherish and call upon
        when they are grown and on their own.

Remind me, Lord,
    to always take advantage of every opportunity I get
        to draw us all closer together.

Developing Love of Family

I see and hear about so much disharmony
    in adult families—
        about brothers arguing
        and sisters not speaking to one another.

Oh, Lord, please let my children
            grow up really loving each other.

Give me the ability to teach them
    to truly respect and like one another—
        and to always be sincerely concerned
            about each other's feelings and well-being.

Give them the understanding they need
    to be able to accept each other's faults and weaknesses
        and not ridicule or make fun of each other.

Let them learn to always be generous enough
    to appreciate and praise each other's assets and talents
        and never be envious of one another.

Give them the ability to be genuinely proud
    of each other's accomplishments
        and achievements.

Dear Lord, let me also be instrumental
    in teaching them how to have fun
        with each other—
            and to really value the friendship
            that is theirs to share.

Oh, Lord, let us all realize
        just how lucky we are to have each other.

NINE

Facing Adolescence

Disciplining Teenagers

I remember when I used to think
    that parenting was hard
        when my children were toddlers—
but now that they're teenagers,
        my job seems overwhelmingly difficult.

I try so hard to keep up with their roller-coaster emotions
        and the continuous crises in their lives.

Oh, Lord, give me the wisdom
    and the patience I need
        to know how to deal with them and all their concerns.

Help me to understand them better than I do.

However, don't let my attempts to understand them
        ever lead me into lowering my expectations of them.

Let me remember, Lord,
        that it's more important now than ever
            to stand firm and set boundaries for them.

Let me also remember that we parents
    can support each other
        when our kids push for too much leniency.

Help us all to realize
    that, although our children will never admit
        to needing rules and restrictions,
    our rules often help to make their lives
        and their decisions easier.

Lord, please help our teenagers become
    responsible adults, who may someday actually
        thank us for the boundaries we have set for them.

Keeping Them on the Right Path

I pray, Lord, that you will protect my children
    from getting involved in the many temptations
      that are out there beckoning to them.

I constantly try to teach them what's right—
    to say "no" to drinking and drugs,
    to avoid friends who may be a bad influence,
    to be responsible and moral
      in dealing with their adolescent urges.

I hope they'll always listen to me,
    but who knows what they may choose to do,
    or let themselves be talked into doing,
      when they're out.

Dear Lord, I'll try my hardest
    to keep my lines of communication open to them
    and to set a good example for them to follow—
    but, Lord, I also need your help.

I want to place them in your hands, dear Father.

Stay near them and give them
    the wisdom, the strength, and the ability
    to say "no" to mind-altering substances
      and conscience-numbing attitudes,
    to say "no" to friends who urge them
      to be reckless and foolish,
    to stop themselves when they are tempted
      to do something they know is wrong.

I need you, Lord, to watch over them
    and keep them on the right path.

Teaching About Sex

Lord, give me the wisdom I need to teach my children
the right attitudes toward sex.

Give me the ability to teach them
that the act of love
is a sacred and beautiful gift from you—
and not the selfish, irresponsible function
portrayed by today's movies, books, and songs.

Help me, Lord, to always set a good example for them
and to be able to instill in them a sense of respect
not only for themselves and their own bodies
but also for those they happen to care for
and be attracted to,
for those who will have to live with
the emotional—and possibly physical—
consequences of my teenagers' choices.

Lord, help my children develop the attitude
that it's all right to say "no"
to intimacy before marriage.

Let them learn to view sex
not as a means to popularity,
but as a serious, unselfish, and commitment-bound
expression of their love—
a gift to be used as you meant it to be used.

Keep them in your care, Lord, and help them
whenever they are tempted to do something
that is foolish and irresponsible.

Choosing Friends Wisely

Lord, help me to teach my children
    how to choose their friends wisely.

They want so much to be part of a group,
    but in their need for acceptance by their peers,
        they sometimes choose friends
            whom I find quite unacceptable.

I realize that it's easy to alienate my children
    by being overly critical of their friends.

Help me to always deal with their choices
    with patience, sensitivity, and tact.

Dear Lord, I pray that you give them
    the wisdom and understanding they need
        to develop friendships that are good for them.

Protect them from getting involved
    with friends who will hurt them—
        friends who are irresponsible and inconsiderate—
        friends who have views
            that are not in keeping with our family values.

Guide them, Lord, and let them be attracted
    to friends who are not only kind and caring,
    but who also live according to good moral principles.

Let them be wise enough to choose friends
    who will ultimately help them
        to become better people.

TEN

Preparing for Life

Instilling a Sense of Mission

I often wonder what will become of my children
            when they grow up and become adults.
      Will they be personally successful?
      Will they be kind and charitable?
      Will they become good, responsible,
            contributing members of society?

Help me, Lord, to be able to foster
            a sense of mission in my children.

Let me be able to show them
      that we were each put on this earth to do a job—
            to fulfill a specific purpose or mission.

Let them be able to understand
      that each of us is special and unique—
            and although we can't all be world-movers,
      each of us—in our own special way—
            can contribute something
                  to make our world just a little bit better.

Let me be able to inspire them
      to find their own special niche in life—
            and be willing to work hard to fulfill it.

And help us all to remember our main purpose in life,
Lord—
      we are here on this earth
            to know, to love, and to serve you
                  through knowing, loving, and serving others.

Supporting Their Dreams

Lord, let me be able to inspire my children
    to hold on to their dreams and goals
        with determination, persistence, and confidence.

Give each of them the ability and the desire
    to strive eagerly and confidently for their dreams—
        to always work hard for them
            and not be deterred by occasional failures.

Let them realize that,
    although dreams are sometimes hard to attain,
        with your help, they are not unattainable.

Give me the wisdom I need, Lord,
    to be able to guide and help them—
        always encouraging and praising,
            but not pushing and pressuring.

And don't let me ever forget
    that these dreams must be *their* dreams, Lord—
        not mine.

I must admit
    that there are times when I'm really tempted
        to steer them into doing things my way.

Remind me, Lord,
    to always listen to their desires and preferences—
        and then do all I can to help them
            to fulfill their dreams and goals
                according to their own wishes.

Imparting My Most Precious Gifts

As a parent, Lord, I have the power to give my children
some of the most precious gifts on earth.

Let me be able to give them the gift of positive thinking,
so they may have the ability to face life with
a sense of satisfaction, contentment, and gratitude.

Let me be able to give them the gift of flexibility,
so they will never be afraid
of all the changes and challenges
they will meet in the course of their lives.

Let me be able to give them the gift of self-confidence,
so they may have the ability
to face the daily events in their lives
with a sense of security and self-worth.

Let me be able to give them the gift of joy,
so they may always know how to take full pleasure
in all the little things of life.

Let me be able to give them the gift of wonder,
so they may always view your beautiful world
with a sense of appreciation, curiosity, and awe.

Let me be able to give them the gift of love,
so they may always have enough love in them
to give to others.

Developing a Sense of Humor

Give me the ability, Lord, to foster
    a good sense of humor in my children.

I often tend to take life—and myself—too seriously.

Don't let me pass this too-sober—
    and often joyless and spiritless—
        attitude on to my children.

Let me be able to teach them how to always see
    the lighter, brighter side of life.

And let us be able to learn together
    how to share our laughter with each other.

Let us learn how to be able to laugh at ourselves—
    even at our own mistakes and weaknesses.

However, don't let us ever become so insensitive—
    or so mean—
    as to make others the butt of our jokes.

Remind us, Lord, to always be careful
    to laugh with—not at—others.

Dear Lord, I ask you to grant each of us the ability
    to see the humor in everyday life—
    and to always enjoy our lives together
    to the full.

Blessing for My Children's Future

Lord, I pray that my children will be wise enough
   to make choices that will enable them
      to find happiness and fulfillment in their lives.

I ask you, Lord, to guide them
         in their choice of vocations.
   Let them choose careers that
         not only will provide them with satisfying lives
      but also will help them
         to make a contribution to the world
            in which they and their children will live.

Guide them, Lord, in their choice of partners.
   Let them be able to find spouses
      who are loyal, kind, and responsible—
      who will give them love, support,
            and lifelong commitment.

Bless them with strong, healthy children of their own,
   and grant them the ability to successfully pass
      their knowledge, their goodness, and their love
         on to their children.

Give them the grace of joyful commitment
   in the single life
      if that is their path.

Dear Lord, let them all live good and meaningful lives—
   lives that are blessed with family and friends,
      who will bring them happiness and fulfillment.

ELEVEN

Dealing with Other People

Developing Concern for Others

Lord, give me the wisdom and the ability
  to inspire my children
    to be sincerely concerned about other people.

Let me know how to encourage them
  to grow out of their childish self-centeredness
    and develop an attitude of thoughtfulness
      and helpfulness toward others.

Remind me to always set a good example for them—
  by giving them the opportunity to see and help me
    give aid and support to neighbors and relatives—
  by encouraging them to visit and comfort
    the sick, the lonely, and the needy—
  by including them in the donating
    of our time and resources to charitable causes.

Let me be able to inspire them to feel deeply concerned
  about those who are less fortunate than they are.

And give me the ability to make them understand
  that we all have an obligation
  to share our advantages,
    our support,
    our aid,
    and our friendship with others.

Help me, Lord, to be able to instill in them
  not only a sense of community and service
    but also a deep sense of awareness
      that we are all each other's keepers.

Instilling Respect for Authority

Lord, let me be able to foster
    a sense of respect for authority in my children.

There have been times
    when I've caught myself criticizing
        people who are in charge of things.

Let me make sure that I don't do or say anything
    that would undermine the respect my children have
        for the people who try to work with them—
    their teachers, their coaches, their pastors,
        our law enforcement officers.

Let me always go out of my way
    to support these people—
        and to always work with them in their attempts
        to teach and discipline my children.

Lord, give me the ability to teach my children
    how to truly understand and appreciate the good things
        that those who are in authority
           are trying to do for them.

Avoiding Prejudice

Help me, Lord, to avoid instilling
    any type of prejudice in my children.

I sometimes forget myself and say things
    that show my disapproval of others
        merely because they are different from me.

Let me be careful to always avoid
    saying or doing anything
        that would prompt my children
            to look down on other people.

Give me the wisdom I need to raise them to be
    kind, understanding, and compassionate individuals,
        who not only accept the differences in others
        but also are able to find something to admire
            in all these differences.

Give me the ability, Lord, to teach my children
    how to sincerely love, respect,
        and be friendly to all kinds of people.

Being Kind to Others

Lord, give me the ability to teach my children
    to always be kind to others.

I must admit that there are times when I find myself
    being unkind and critical of other people.

Don't let me be guilty of setting
    a bad example for them to follow.

Let me be able to teach them how wrong it is
    to join in when their companions
        are being mean and making fun of others.

Let them be able to understand that such behavior
    is not only terribly hurtful
        but can also make them responsible
            for inciting revenge and violence in others.

Help me, Lord, to teach my children to treat others
    as they would like others to treat them.

Dear Lord, give me the wisdom I need
    to know how to raise my children to be
        concerned, friendly, and genuinely nice people.

TWELVE

Special Situations

Blessing

I pray, Lord,
  that you will always keep my children in your care.

Grant that they may enjoy
  good physical, mental, and emotional health
    throughout their lives.
  Keep their bodies strong—
    their attitudes positive—
      and their values solid and true.

Give them the ability to face life head-on
  and meet all their challenges with a confidence
    and eagerness that allows them
  not only to achieve their dreams
  but also to fully enjoy the road they choose to travel.

Fill their lives with people who will always love them,
    support them, and inspire them.

Dear Lord, draw them close to you—
    and let their faith in you—
      and in the important things of life—
        grow stronger each day.

I pray, Lord, that they will grow up to be
    genuinely kind individuals,
      who are filled with love, caring, and goodness.

For a Child Doing Poorly in School

Lord, (*Name*) is not doing too well in school.

Please help my child to deal with
   feelings of discouragement and failure.

Dear Lord, give my child the wisdom
   to understand and absorb those subjects
      that are especially difficult.

Fill this child
   not only with a strong desire and eagerness to learn,
   but also with a willingness to study more diligently.

I also pray, Lord, that you give the teachers
   the wisdom, patience, and understanding
      to help my child through this difficult time.

Teach me, Lord, how to work with them
   in providing my child
      the aid and support necessary for success.

And keep reminding me, Lord, to always praise
   not just the achievements
   but also the effort my child puts
      into attaining them.

For a Troubled Child

Dear Lord, this child of mine is such
a troubled and unhappy person.

It's really difficult to watch (*Name*)
react so negatively—so sadly—to life.

Please help my child, dear Lord,
and don't let the daily trials and occasional failures
cause so much discouragement and sadness.

Give this child strength and understanding
to face the stresses of daily living
with more courage, faith, and confidence.

Help bring about a change of outlook
and a more positive and cheerful attitude toward life.

O Lord, give me the wisdom I need
to teach my child how to lighten up
and see the joys in daily life.

Let me be able to show this child
how to get more pleasure and satisfaction
out of accomplishments, relationships,
and all the small everyday things of life.

Help my child, Lord, to develop
a more contented, more joyful attitude toward living.

For a Sick Child

Lord, please help (*Name*) to get well soon.

I'm afraid that my child doesn't have
                   much patience
         with illness and discomfort.

I must admit that there are times, too,
      when I don't have much patience
         with all the crabbiness and the constant demands.

It's really exhausting to care for a sick child, Lord.

Give me the patience and the energy I need
      to nurse, to comfort, to soothe pains—
         and to do whatever is necessary
            to bring about good health.

Dear Lord, I ask you to give my child
      the strength to deal patiently
         with all the discomforts of this illness.
         And I pray that you will bless my child
            with a good and speedy recovery.

For the Safety of My Children

Lord, I ask that you always keep my children safe
      when they're away from home.

When they're out, I worry not only about accidents
      but also about all the bad influences
         and dangerous circumstances they may encounter
         away from the safety of our home.

Dear God,
      I would like to place my children in your hands.

I pray that you will stay near them, keep them safe—
      and help them to always behave
         as I have taught them to behave.

Let your angels watch over them constantly
      and keep them from all harm.

I pray, Lord, that my children and their companions
      return home safely.

For a Child with Special Needs

Life is so much harder for this child of mine, Lord.

Sometimes I feel so sorry for (*Name*)
   and desperately wish that I could make life easier—
      but I can't.

As a result, I often catch myself
   being overly helpful and protective.

Remind me, Lord,
   that I do my child no favor by behaving this way.
      Give me the wisdom and understanding I need
   to do what is best for my child.

Help me do all I can to prepare this child
   for a life that will most likely
      be harder than the average life.

Teach me how to promote the development
   of self-reliance, faith, joy, independence,
      and an eagerness for living fully.

Don't let me ever say or do anything
   that might foster self-pity in my child.

Dear Lord, I ask you to grant me the ability
   to instill an attitude toward life
      that is both positive and confident,
   so that my child may find
      joy and fulfillment in all the hopes and dreams
         that are possible for this child to attain.

For a Child Leaving Home

It's so hard for me, Lord, to see my child,
   who seems so young and vulnerable,
      all grown up and ready to leave home.

I keep wondering if I've done a good enough job
   preparing this child to go out and face life
      without my daily guidance and care.

I guess there's not much I can do right now, Lord,
   but to place this young person in your hands
      to keep safe, well, wise, and good.

Dear Lord, I ask you to give this child of mine
   the wisdom to always make good decisions—
   and the strength that will be needed
      to avoid being influenced
         by the bad judgment and false beliefs of others.

I also ask you to grant my child the ability
   to always stay true to our family's views and values.

Help my child, dear Lord, to always stay close to you
   and to know that you and I are always available
      to provide all the help, the support, and the love
         that this child may need from us.

For the Wisdom to Parent a Grown Child

After guiding my children
    through all their years of growing up,
        it's really hard for me to adjust
            to being a parent of an adult.

It's all so different now, Lord.
    I definitely need your guidance
        in this new stage of my life.

Remind me, Lord,
    to always treat my children as grownups,
        and let me learn to respect their independence.

Give me the wisdom I need
    to know just when I should offer advice
    and when I should hold back
        and accept their way of handling things.

Remind me to always carefully watch what I say and do
    so that I may never be guilty
        of undermining their confidence—
        of injuring their relationships—
        or of interfering in areas where
            my interference can impair our relationship.

Let me be able to help them when they ask for help—
    to wisely advise them when they ask for advice—
    to support them when they need support—
    to comfort them when they need comfort—
    and to love them—no matter what they do.

Help me, Lord, to always be a wise,
    helpful, and
        loving parent.

For My Children Who Are Becoming Parents

What a blessing, Lord!
   I'm going to become a grandparent!
      Thank you for bringing me
         to this wonderful stage in life.

I ask you, Lord, to bless my loved ones
         with a normal, healthy, and beautiful child.

Watch over these precious expectant parents
    and help them to prepare themselves
    for parenthood.
I wonder if they really understand just how greatly
       their lives will be affected by this new life.

Don't let them be overwhelmed by their responsibility.

Let them be able to handle this enormous life-change
   without losing the love,
     the intimacy,
       and the happiness that they now enjoy.

Dear Lord, I ask you to give them
   the wisdom,
   the patience,
   and the strength they'll need
     to be able to cope with all the hassles of parenting.

Stay close to them always
     and guide them in their efforts to bring up
       good, happy, and loving children.

For the Good of My Children

Bless my children, Lord,
    and fill them with your love and your grace.

Fill them with wisdom so they may always know
    how to make the right choices in life.

Fill them with courage so they may not become
    overwhelmed by the burdens of life.

Fill them with determination so they may never be
    tempted to give up easily when things go wrong.

Fill them with acceptance so they may know how to
accept and live through
    whatever happens in their lives.

Fill them with a sense of satisfaction so they may never
    be envious of others or discontented with their lives.

Fill them with understanding
    so they may know how to accept
    the faults, weaknesses, and differences in others.

Fill them with kindness so they may always
    treat others with gentleness, concern, and caring.

Fill them with forgiveness so they may never
    waste their time on anger, resentment, or revenge.

Fill them with a sense of purpose
    so they may always meet their challenges
    and successfully fulfill their missions in life.

Fill them with faith so they may never
    become prisoners of doubt or despair.

Fill them with your peace so they may always
feel secure and confident and unafraid.

Fill them with love so they may always
possess an abundance of love to give to others.

Fill them with your presence so they may never
feel alone or frightened or helpless.

Fill them with a sense of joy
so they may appreciate your gift of life
and always live it to the full.